My Practice Workbook

Handwriting

with Kids Club

Ages 5-7

This book belongs to: ....

Fill in your certificate when you have completed this book.

I completed this book on

Date: ....

Signature: ....

Well done

Advice for parents and carers

This book is designed for children to complete on their own, but you may like to work with them for the first few pages.

- Don't get your child to do too much at once. A 'little and often' approach is a good way to start.
- Your child should work through the book unit by unit.
- Reward your child with lots of praise and encouragement.
- Talk to your child about what they have learnt and what they can do.
- The '**Get ready**' section provides a gentle warm-up for the topic covered on the page.
- The '**Let's practise**' section consolidates understanding of the topic. Your child will need a notebook for some of the activities.
- The '**Tips from teachers**' are written by practising classroom teachers. They give useful advice on specific topics or skills, to deepen your child's understanding and confidence and to help you help your child.

Handwriting

All literacy work in schools comes under the broad headings of speaking, listening, reading and writing. Each of these headings has a number of 'strands', which are taught systematically. This series of books aims to support the work your child does at school.

Handwriting comes under strand 12, which is 'Presentation'. By the end of Year 2, most children should be able to:

- write legibly, using upper and lower case
- letters appropriately within words, and
- observing correct spacing within and between words
- form and use the four basic handwriting joins
- word process short narrative and non-narrative texts.

If you have access to a computer at home then you will be able to give your child a chance to improve these skills. If you do not have a computer, then you could visit your local library to enquire about computer resources available locally.

Hachette UK's policy is to use papers that are natural, renewable and recyclable products and made from wood grown in well-managed forests and other controlled sources. The logging and manufacturing processes are expected to conform to the environmental regulations of the country of origin.

Orders: please contact Hachette UK Distribution, Hely Hutchinson Centre, Milton Road, Didcot, Oxfordshire, OX11 7HH. Telephone: +44 (0)1235 827827. Email education@hachette.co.uk Lines are open from 9 a.m. to 5 p.m., Monday to Friday. You can also order through our website: www.hoddereducation.co.uk

ISBN: 9781398388864

© Richard Cooper 2023
Tips from teachers © Najoud Ensaff 2023
First published in 2013. This edition published in 2023 by Hodder Education, an Hachette UK Company, Carmelite House, 50 Victoria Embankment, London EC4Y 0DZ

All rights reserved. Apart from any use permitted under UK copyright law, no part of this publication may be reproduced or transmitted in any form or by any means, electronic or mechanical, including photocopying and recording, or held within any information storage and retrieval system, without permission in writing from the publisher or under licence from the Copyright Licensing Agency Limited. Further details of such licences (for reprographic reproduction) may be obtained from the Copyright Licensing Agency Limited, www.cla.co.uk

Typeset and printed in the UK. Character illustrations by Lisa Hunt from the Bright Agency. Other illustrations by Fakenham Prepress Solutions. A catalogue record for this title is available from the British Library.

Impression number   10 9 8 7 6 5 4 3 2 1
Year   2027 2026 2025 2024 2023

MIX
Paper | Supporting responsible forestry
FSC™ C104740
www.fsc.org

Contents

Advice for parents and carers 2

Developing handwriting skills 4

Developing motor skills 5

Welcome to Kids Club! 6

Personal profile 7

Pencil movements 8

Long ladder letters (1) 10

Long ladder letters (2) 12

The one-armed robot (1) 14

The one-armed robot (2) 16

The curly caterpillar (1) 18

The curly caterpillar (2) 20

Zigzag letter 22

The four letter formations 24

Joining patterns (1) 26

Joining patterns (2) 28

Joined-up writing 30

Practice sheet 32

Colour the stars as you go!

Developing handwriting skills

There is no single recommended style for handwriting. Each school will probably have its own handwriting policy which will aim to teach your child to write in a way that is legible, fast and fluent. This should involve a style that enables your child to join the letters easily. If a child finds the act of handwriting difficult, he or she is unlikely to evolve into a confident and expressive writer in the future.

You are entitled to see a school's handwriting policy if you so wish. It should include something resembling the following:

- the school's aims and objectives for handwriting

- how the school will cover the curriculum with reference to the Frameworks for Teaching

- how the school proposes to teach letter formation and joining. There may be agreed names for the different formations, which should be known by all teachers, teaching assistants and pupils

- how left-handed children are catered for

- how the school's preferred style of handwriting is communicated to parents and carers

- which materials the school will use and when the children will be expected to use pens or pencils

- how the school caters for children with special educational needs (SEN)

- how much freedom children will have to develop their own individual styles of writing.

Developing motor skills

There are plenty of activities your child can do at home to develop his or her fine motor control. This is the term used to describe smaller movements (usually with the fingers and hands). Teachers have noted that some boys develop fine motor skills more slowly than girls.

Until your child has developed a fair degree of fine motor control it is best to avoid using books or worksheets apart from those the teacher is using in the classroom.

Here are some activities you can encourage your child to do at home to help improve his or her fine motor skills:

- sewing and weaving

- playing with construction toys

- cooking; including cutting and peeling (adult supervision required!)

- sieving, pouring and modelling in a sand and water tray

- using tweezers to pick up small objects, and scissors to cut out shapes and patterns

- playing with clay and modelling dough. Children can practise making letter shapes and numbers

- using fingers and thick brushes to paint the four letter formations on pieces of paper. You will find these four formations in this book.

Above all, allow your child to enjoy exploring the many ways of making their mark!

Welcome to Kids Club!

Hi, readers. My name's Charlie and I run Kids Club with my friend Abbie. Kids Club is an after-school club that is very similar to one somewhere near you.

We'd love you to come and join our club and see what we get up to!

I'm Abbie and I run Kids Club with Charlie. Let's meet the kids who will work with you on the activities in this book.

My name's Jamelia. I look forward to Kids Club every day. The sports and games are my favourites, especially on Kids Camp in the school holidays.

Hi, I'm Megan. I've made friends with all the children at Kids Club. I like the outings and trips we go on the best.

Hello, my name's Jae. Kids Club is a great place to chill out after school. My best friend is Alfie – everyone knows Alfie!

I'm Amina. I like to do my homework at Kids Club. Charlie and Abbie are always very helpful. We're like one big happy family.

Greetings, readers. My name's Alfie! Everybody knows me here. Come and join our club. We'll have a great time together!

Now you've met us all, tell us something about yourself.

All the children filled in a '**Personal profile**' when they joined. There's one on the next page for you to complete.

Personal profile

DRAW A PICTURE OF YOURSELF HERE

Name: Elliott Glenister

Age: 5

School: FAIRHOUSE

Home town: BASILDON

Pets: _____

My favourite:

★ book is _____,

★ film is _____,

★ food is _____,

★ sport is _____.

My hero is _____ because _____
_____

When I grow up I want to be a _____

If I could be king or queen for the day, the first thing I would do is _____
_____.

If I could be any animal for a day I would be a _____
_____.

Colour the star when you complete the page.

Pencil movements

These snails have left a trail. See if you can follow them.

⭐ **Get ready**

First trace the lines with your finger. Then use a pencil. Start on the red dot and follow the blue arrow.

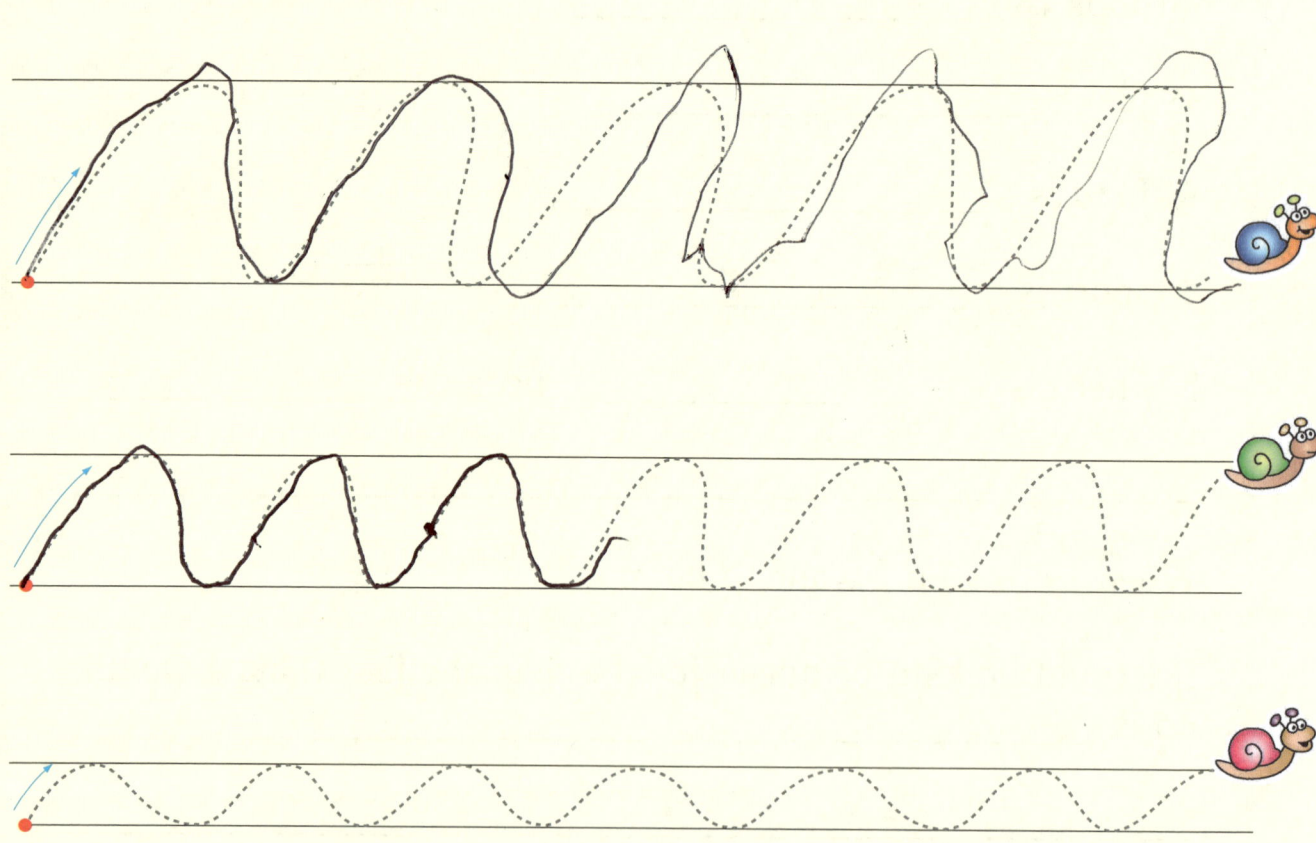

Colour the star when you complete the page.

⭐ **Let's practise**

Now trace round the outside of these shapes with your finger. Then do the same with a pencil. Start on the red dot and follow the blue arrow. Keep the pencil on the paper until you complete each one.

Tips from teachers

Most people find the best way to hold a pencil is to put your thumb on one side and your second finger on the other. Rest the pencil on your third finger and write. It will get easier with practice!

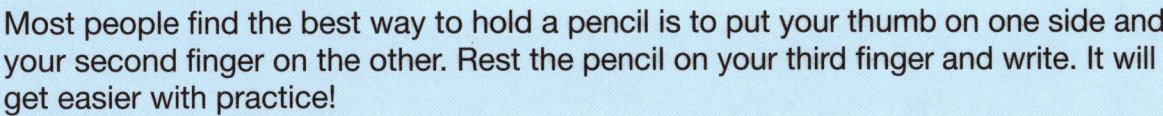

Colour the star when you complete the page.

Long ladder letters (1)

I'll show you how to write the 'long ladder' letters. The best example of the long ladder letter is **l**.

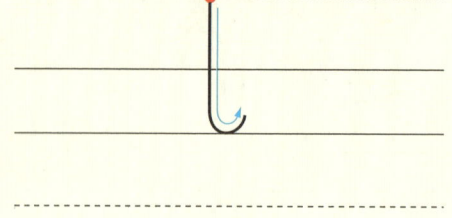

Now we can practise **i** and **j**. They start at the top and go down and off in another direction.

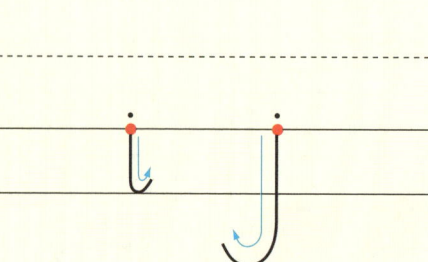

 **Get ready**

Trace the lines with your pencil in the direction of the arrows. Start at the red dot. Then write the letters yourself across the page.

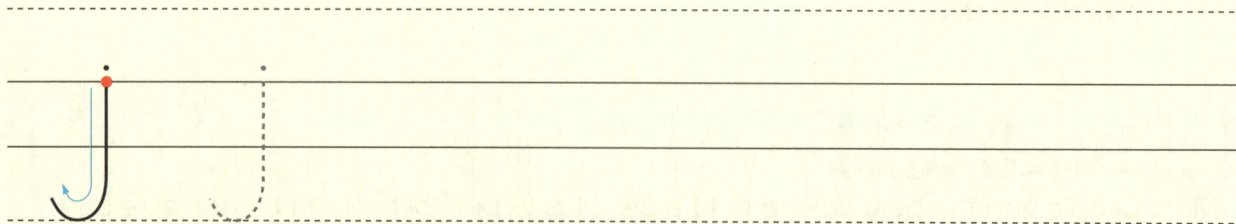

Colour the star when you complete the page.

 **Let's practise**

Trace the lines with your pencil in the direction of the arrows. Then write the letters yourself across the page. For 'il' and 'li', add the dot for the 'i' after writing both the letters.

Tips from teachers

Practise the letters in the air with your second finger so that you know which direction to go in before you use your pencil. This will help you a lot!

Colour the star when you complete the page.

Long ladder letters (2)

Now we can practise **t**, **u** and **y**.

Remember, start at the top, then come down and off in another direction.

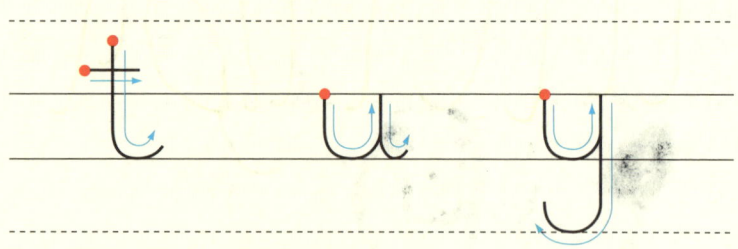

 **Get ready**

Trace the lines with your pencil in the direction of the arrows. Start at the red dot. Then write the letters yourself across the page.

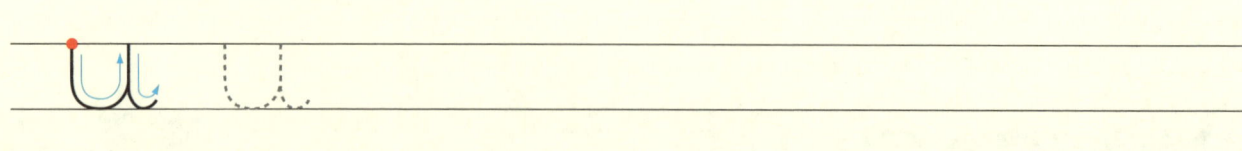

Colour the star when you complete the page.

 **Let's practise**

Trace the lines with your pencil in the direction of the arrows. Then write the letters yourself across the page.

t t

u u

y y

t u t u

t u t u

u t u t

Tips from teachers

Keep practising those letters in the air. Have a few goes with a grown-up – just so you know where to start and end your letters on the page.

Colour the star when you complete the page.

The one-armed robot (1)

I'm going to show you how to write the 'one-armed robot' letters.

The best example of the one-armed robot letter is **r**.

The others are **n**, **m**, **p**, **b**, **h** and **k**. They all start at the top, come down and retrace upwards.

Get ready

Trace the lines with your pencil in the direction of the arrows. Then write the letters yourself across the page.

Colour the star when you complete the page.

Let's practise

Trace the lines with your pencil in the direction of the arrows. Then write the letters yourself across the page.

r r

n n

m m

mn mn

p p

Tips from teachers

The red dot is there to help you. It tells you where to start with your pencil. The arrow shows you which way to go with the pencil once you start.

Colour the star when you complete the page.

The one-armed robot (2)

Now let's try the letters **b**, **h** and **k**.

Let's start with **b**. Remember, start at the top, come down and retrace upwards.

⭐ **Get ready**

Trace the lines with your pencil in the direction of the arrows. Then write the letters yourself across the page.

Colour the star when you complete the page.

 **Let's practise**

Trace the lines with your pencil in the direction of the arrows. Then write the letters yourself across the page.

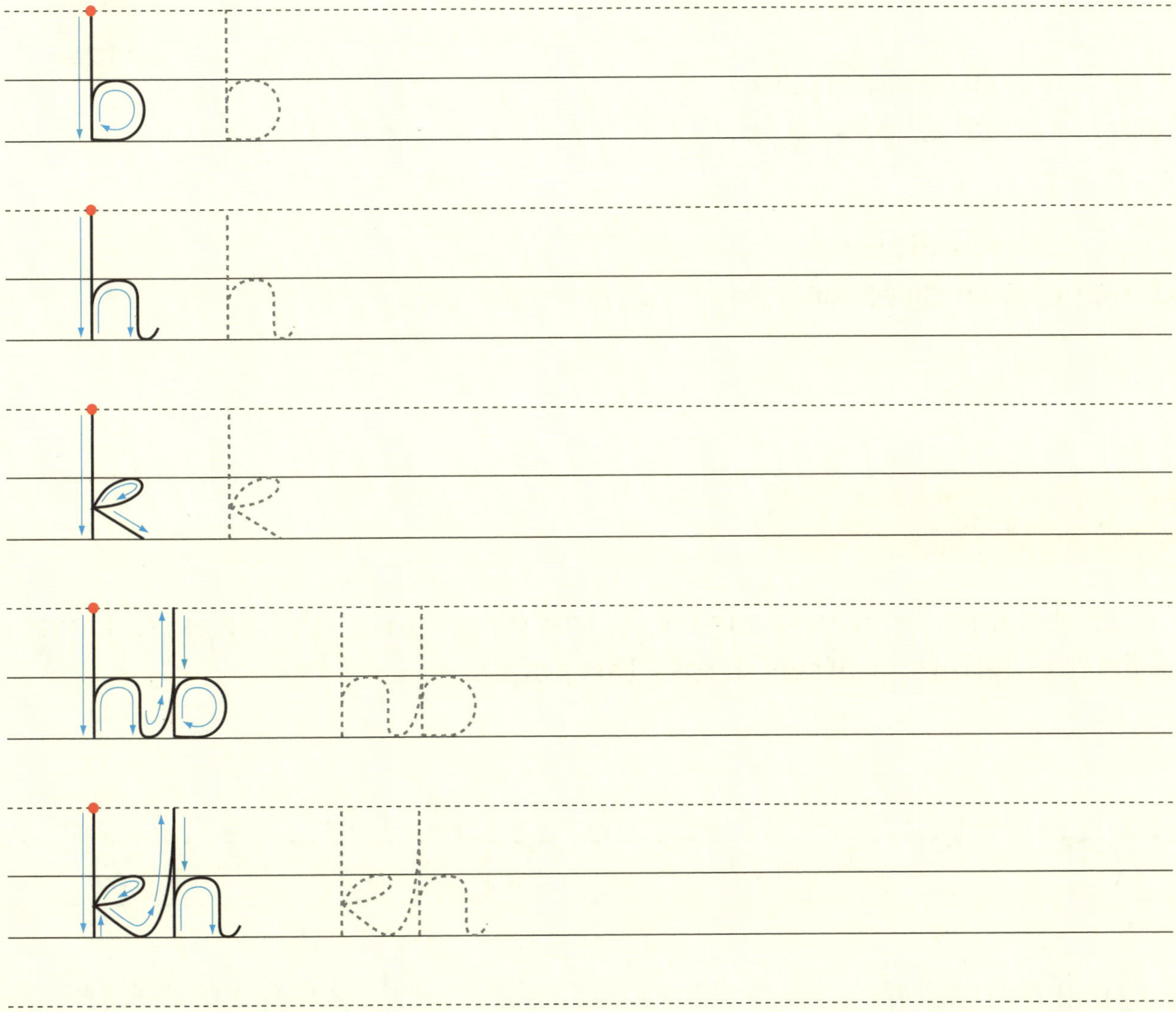

b

h

k

hb

kh

Tips from teachers

Did you notice how these letters have similar shapes? They all go down then around in some way. Kicking 'k' has legs though and 'b' is round – just like your mouth when you say the letter sound 'b'.

Colour the star when you complete the page.

The curly caterpillar (1)

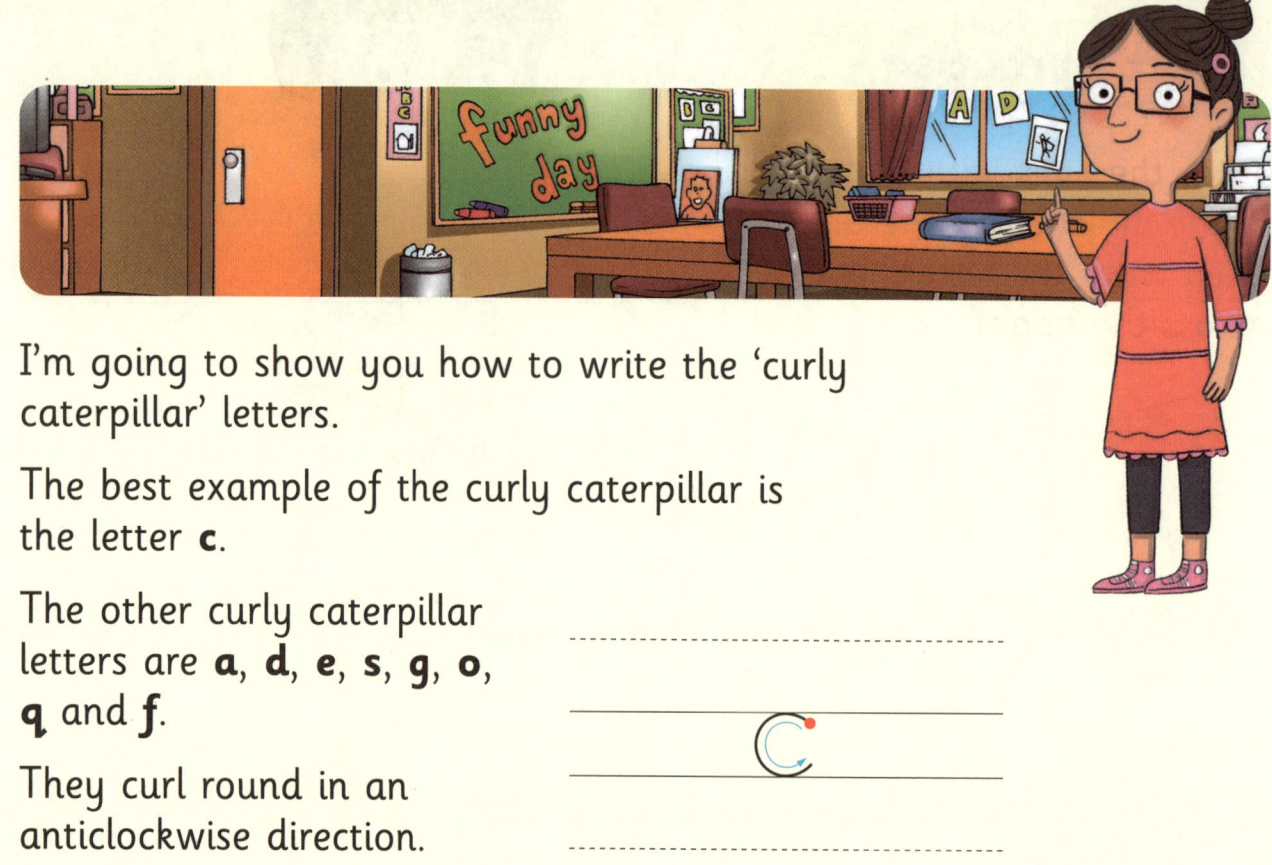

I'm going to show you how to write the 'curly caterpillar' letters.

The best example of the curly caterpillar is the letter **c**.

The other curly caterpillar letters are **a**, **d**, **e**, **s**, **g**, **o**, **q** and **f**.

They curl round in an anticlockwise direction.

⭐ **Get ready**

Trace the lines with your pencil in the direction of the arrows. Then write the letters yourself across the page.

c c   a a

d d   e e

Colour the star when you complete the page.

 **Let's practise**

Trace the lines with your pencil in the direction of the arrows. Then write the letters yourself across the page.

c c

a a

d d

e e

s s

da da

Tips from teachers

Curly 'c' has a shape like the handle of a 'cup', which begins with 'c'. An 'a' is nice and round, just like an apple, which starts with an 'a'.

Colour the star when you complete the page.

The curly caterpillar (2)

Now we can write the letters **g**, **o**, **q** and **f**.

Remember: start by curling round in an anticlockwise direction.

⭐ Get ready

Trace the lines with your pencil in the direction of the arrows. Then write the letters yourself across the page.

Colour the star when you complete the page.

 **Let's practise**

Trace the lines with your pencil in the direction of the arrows. Then write the letters yourself across the page.

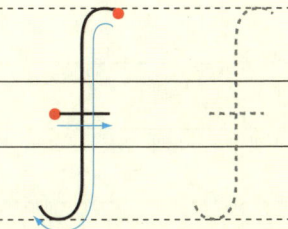

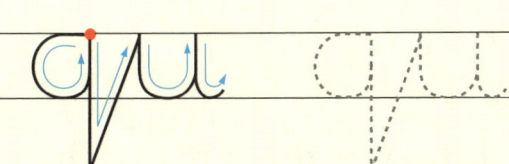

Tips from teachers

g, f and q are special letters. They have tails. Make sure you take your pencil down enough for these letters. Their tails are like roots that go below ground!

Colour the star when you complete the page.

Zigzag letters

It's my turn now! I'm going to show you how to write the 'zigzag' letters.

The best example of a zigzag letter is **z**.

The others are **v**, **w** and **x**.

Zigzag letters change direction.

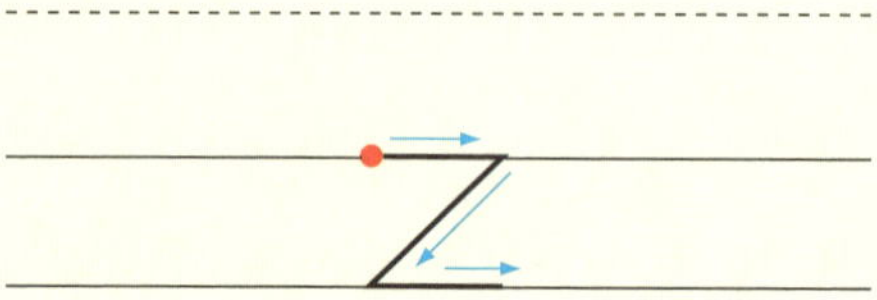

⭐ Get ready

Trace the lines with your pencil in the direction of the arrows. Then write the letters yourself across the page.

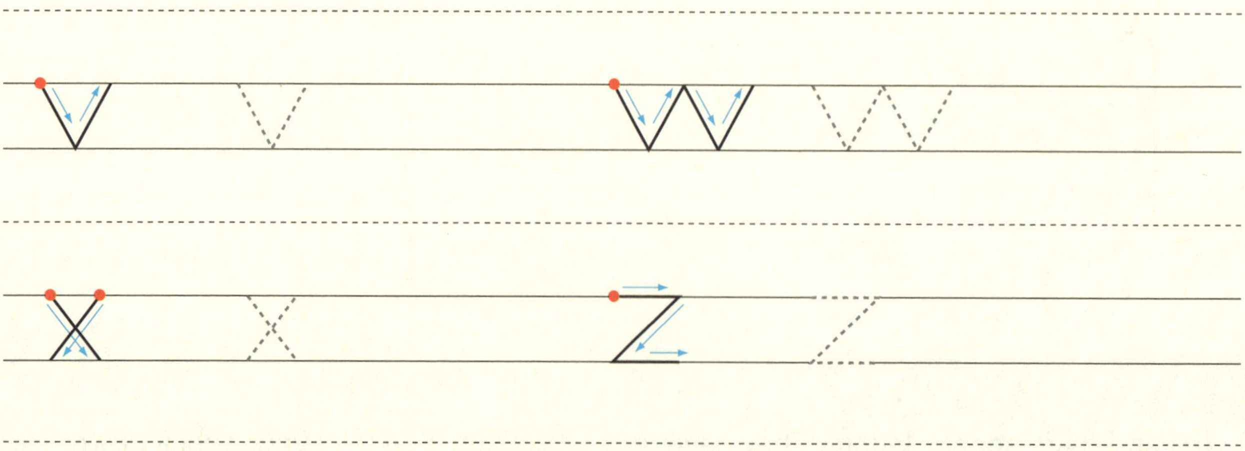

Colour the star when you complete the page.

Let's practise

Trace the lines with your pencil in the direction of the arrows. Then write the letters yourself across the page.

v

w

x

z

Tips from teachers

See if you can watch a clip from a cartoon version of Zorro to spot how this famous bandit shapes his 'Z' for Zorro letters.

Colour the star when you complete the page.

The four letter formations

Let's recap what we have done so far. For each letter, learn the starting point and the movements you make with the pencil.

 Let's practise

Practise the four formations here. Trace the lines with your pencil in the direction of the arrows. Then write the letters yourself across the page.

The long ladder

The one-armed robot

Colour the star when you complete the page.

The curly caterpillar

c c

a a

Zigzag letters

z z

x x

Tips from teachers

Notice how the title of each section gives you a clue about how to shape your letters. Do you think the letter x looks a little like something you've seen before? Use this to help you remember it.

Colour the star when you complete the page.

Joining patterns (1)

Now you can write all the letters, let's practise joining them up. Here are four joining patterns.

 **Let's practise**

Start at the dot. Trace the lines with your pencil in the direction of the arrows. Then copy the pattern across the page.

Diagonal joins. These are the most common joins.

ai   ai

un   un

Diagonal joins into ascenders. These join into letters with tails that go up towards the top of the grid.

ab   ab

it   it

Colour the star when you complete the page.

Horizontal joins. You use this join *after* **o**, **r**, **v** and **w**.

ou ou

wi wi

Horizontal joins into **ascenders**. You use this movement for joins into **b**, **h**, **k**, **l** and **t**.

ot ot

wh wh

Tips from teachers

Remember those finger patterns we did earlier? Try these with your new joined-up letters. This will help you to know how to write the letters with a pencil.

Colour the star when you complete the page.

Joining patterns (2)

Here we are going to look at another joining pattern. But some of the letters don't need to join at all!

 **Let's practise**

Up and over

This join is called the 'up and over'. You use it to join *into* **a**, **c**, **d**, **g**, **o**, **q** and **s**.

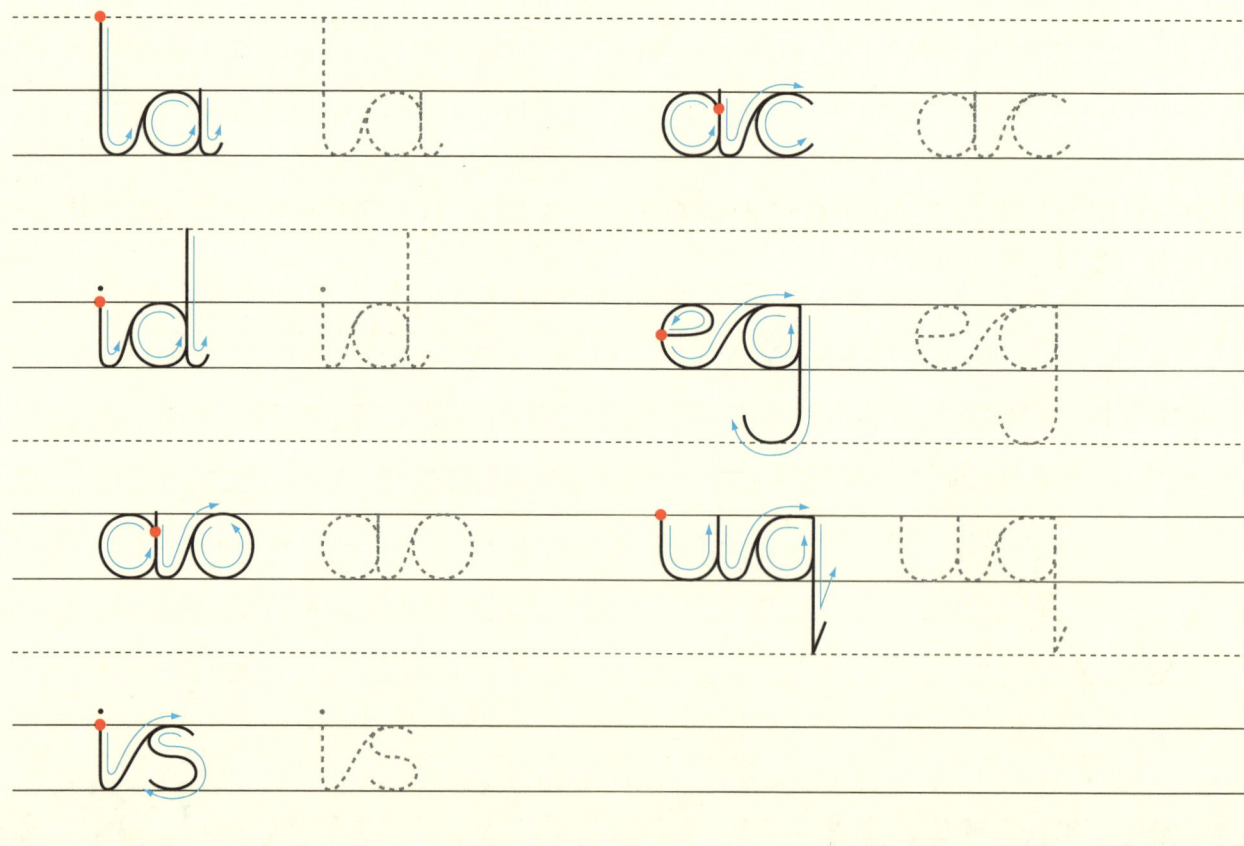

Colour the star when you complete the page.

No joins

You don't normally join at all after these letters: **g**, **j**, **x**, **y**, **z**, **b** and **p**. Capital letters *never* join.

ga ga je je

xa xa

yo yo

zap zap

beg beg

pup pup

Tips from teachers

The *up and over* join that you are shaping here is just like going up and over a mountain. Imagine that you climbing a mountain as you write. This will make it more fun and easier to remember that you need to go up and over!

Colour the star when you complete the page.

Joined-up writing

Now you can practise your writing skills!

 **Get ready**

Everyone in the club has written sentences or phrases for you to copy. Write them as neatly as you can on page 32. Here are some tips.

- Write on the lines.

- Keep the bits of the letters that sit on the line the same size.

- Keep your 'ascenders' and 'descenders' the same size and level with each other. (These are the 'stalks' or 'tails' of letters like **h** and **p**.)

Colour the star when you complete the page.

 **Let's practise**

Write as neatly as you can and take pride in your work!

Easy peezy lemon squeezy.

Practice makes perfect.

The last sentence uses all the letters of the alphabet.

The quick brown fox jumps over the lazy dog.

Tips from teachers

If you find looking back to the words on pages 30–31 a bit difficult as you write, get a grown up to photocopy page 32, or use a page of handwriting paper for you to write on.

Colour the star when you complete the page.

Practice sheet

32

Colour the star when you complete the page.